Underground Clwyd

The Armchair Explorers' Guide

A pictorial expedition into the
nether regions of Northeast Wales

by
CRIS EBBS

©2000

Published by Gordon Emery, 27 Gladstone Road, Chester, CH1 4BZ
Printed by MFP Design & Print, Stretford, Manchester M32 OJT

On Zander`s Mega Matt, produced from 50% recycled fibre and 10% minimum de-inked recycled.

Cover photo

Limestone Mine at Hendre

Mining has created some large caverns in this area, the cover photo shows a typical example.
Mining ceased in the 1960s and most of the equipment was removed, but there are several sites where miners took rests or tea breaks. Here they left old newspapers, cigarette packets and even old boots which remain undisturbed today (see page 12).

(Photo: Martyn Farr)

Acknowledgements

I should like to thank RJB Mining (Point-of-Ayr Colliery), Martin Lloyd (Lloyd`s Quarries), the National Museum of Wales, Tony Pearce (Grange Caverns Military Museum), Martin Pitt (photographer) and the Royal Commission on the Ancient and Historical Monuments of Wales who have all allowed me to use their photographs. Thanks also to Fiona of the Clwyd Record Office for her cheerful assistance.

For the use of photos, I am extremely grateful to friends and fellow cavers: Jerry Dobby, Mike Gannon, Selwyn Edwards, Jon Knowles, Bob Roberts, Chris Williams, Graham Woolley, Nick Catford and Martyn Farr.

Fellow members of the Grosvenor Caving Club deserve special thanks. They have provided invaluable assistance on countless trips over the years and posed, sometimes in sub-human conditions, for many underground camera sessions. Stephen Brown deserves a special thank you for offering to read the draft. In so doing he discovered the many errors that I had missed.

Final thanks extend to the many landowners whose kindness has made our explorations and this book possible, and to my wife Pennie and son Craig for their (almost!) limitless tolerance.

Contents

Opposite: Limestone mine at Hendre

INTRODUCTION

As a cave-cum-mine explorer for 25 years, I have witnessed the loss of many of Clwyd's underground sites. Entrances have collapsed or shafts have been filled or capped. Before too many more are lost, it occurred to me that others might like to glimpse, from the comfort of their favourite armchair, some of the sights that sub-surface Clwyd has, or had, to offer.

This is a collection almost entirely of underground photographs, half my own, half kindly donated, which record some of the more interesting underground sites of the area. I apologise for the preponderance of views of caves and lead mines, but they reflect the topics which receive most attention from modern day underground explorers. Neither is it intended to convey a complete picture of Clwyd's nether regions, but is more of a personal selection intended to whet the appetite of the curious. Please forgive the use of the now defunct county name of Clwyd but it is less cumbersome than 'Flintshire and Denbighshire' and its boundaries more neatly encompass the sites mentioned.

It has been estimated that if all of Clwyd's cave and mine passages were placed end to end, they would cover a distance of over 100 miles. About half this figure is currently accessible to those with the necessary equipment and experience. However, please note that entry into some of the sites mentioned is now impossible. Those which are accessible should never be entered unless accompanied by an experienced caver or mine explorer. Due to their nature these sites can be dangerous and may be liable to flooding. Those wishing to know more about Clwyd's underground heritage are advised to contact one of the local caving or mining groups through your local library, or consult the enclosed list of suggested books for further reading. As most of the sites are privately owned, it is necessary to obtain landowners' permission if planning a visit.

Although much time has been spent in checking details, I would be grateful to hear of any errors which must inevitably occur.

I hope this small book offers the reader some insight into the subterranean world far beyond the light of day.

BRIEF BACKGROUND

The very first open passages created beneath Clwyd`s surface were pre-glacial caves. These were formed by the action of peaty, acidic surface water entering tiny cracks or fissures in the native limestone. In time the cracks became larger, eventually forming caves over many thousands of years. As glaciers came and went, some caves became choked with clay and boulders, whilst others continued to increase in size owing to the further action of stream waters. Today there are over 300 caves known in Clwyd, and although the majority of these are only very short, a handful are impressive and extensive cave systems. Nearly all of these systems have been discovered by burrowing cavers in the last 25 years.

In addition to the formation of these caves, man has been responsible for creating a labyrinth of mine workings in the pursuit of minerals. The first known Clwyd workings were the lead mines of the Romans some 2000 years ago, although copper was worked around 3000 years ago beyond Clwyd`s borders at the nearby Great Orme Mines in Llandudno. Following the departure of the Romans, it appears that little, if any, mining was undertaken until around the year 1250 when farmers attempted to supplement their then meagre incomes by working shallow lead veins on a small scale. Sporadic mining continued along these lines until the introduction of gunpowder for blasting around the year 1650. A succession of further technological advances led to the pinnacle of lead production around 1860 and made many mine owners extremely wealthy.

Coal has been mined from the lowland areas of Clwyd for over 600 years. The major factor influencing coal production was the introduction of the steam pump. All the major coal mines extended below sea-level and became impossible to drain efficiently. The first steam pump in North Wales was a Bull Engine, brought in to work at a colliery on the Dee Estuary in the early 1700s. Development of the steam engine into the form known as the Cornish beam engine radically improved conditions in all mines throughout the country, particularly so in Clwyd, as coal to power these engines could be found on the doorstep.

A few large slate mines have been worked near Clwyd`s southern borders, most of which are easily identified by their large surface waste tips, a sight more generally attributed to the Ffestiniog area 30 miles to the southwest. Several other minerals have been extracted by mining from the area, but on a smaller scale than those already mentioned. These include limestone, silica, calcite, iron ore, barytes, fire-clay and cobalt.

Most mines terminally declined during the first half of the 20th century. Today every single Clwyd mine lies idle. The minerals are still in demand but they can now be obtained more cheaply from around the globe. These low prices are frequently achieved by mines where workers, often children, are paid wages so low that it represents modern day slavery. The last of the local mines to close were those of Lloyd`s Spar Mine (stone) at Hendre in 1984, Halkyn (Lead) Mines also at Hendre in 1987 and, of course, Point of Ayr Colliery in 1996. It is perhaps sad to think that the greatest testament to the achievement of countless generations of miners is the empty workings they leave behind - out of sight and beyond most people's imagination.

As you browse through the following pages, spare a thought for those who lived and those who died by the light of a tallow candle.

1.   STONE MINES

Stone mining in Clwyd encompassed the extraction of limestone, spar (calcite), silica and sandstone. Mined limestone was used chiefly by the chemical industry in the production of fertilisers or as an ingredient in glass making. Spar or white calcite was commonly used as pebble-dash. Silica has been used as an additive in the manufacture of fireclay and as the abrasive constituent in the well known household product 'VIM', and sandstone has been mined for use as general building stone.

The surface quarrying of limestone is now a well established feature of Clwyd`s economy. Fifty years ago, quarrying was a comparatively small scale affair. In recent years it has grown beyond all recognition. Modern extraction rates are many times greater than those of fifty years ago. A typical limestone quarry may now remove one or two million tonnes a year. Little wonder then, that the local population take more than a passing interest in their activities. However, not all stone extraction leaves such an obvious impression upon the landscape: about a dozen Clwyd quarries have been developed beneath the surface. In one case it has proved economical to raise stone from a depth of almost 250 metres beneath Halkyn Mountain.

The workings created by stone mining can be both extensive and spacious. They frequently take the form of a series of adjoining chambers containing, every few metres, pillars of rock left in place to support the roof: a system known as pillar and stall working. In a stone mine near Mold in the 1950s, a manager was under pressure to meet production figures and decided to remove a few of these pillars against the advice of his workers. Predictably, several chambers collapsed and it was more by luck than judgement that no-one was injured.

Grange Caverns, Holywell
The entrance in 1979

A series of chambers covering a hectare were mined above the old A55 road at Holway near Holywell. Mining began in the early 1800s and ended in 1887. The stone was conveyed down a steeply inclined tramway to Greenfield from where it was shipped to Liverpool for use in the construction of the South Docks.

At the outbreak of World War Two, the caverns were taken over by the Ministry of Defence to house 11,000 tons of bombs, amongst which were the famous Barnes Wallis "Bouncing Bombs" used to destroy the Möhne and Eder dams in Germany. >>>>>

Grange Caverns
British 5.5 Howitzer weighing 5.75 tons, range 10 miles

From 1979 the caverns housed a collection of old military vehicles. Over 70 of these were displayed 20–30 metres below the surface when the site was known as Grange Cavern Military museum. It also contained one of the largest badge, button and medal collections in the UK dating back to the 1700s. A "NAAFI Cafe" was constructed together with a fully licensed auditorium with seating for 100. In spite of its popularity and the unusual nature of the venue, it eventually closed in 1989. Today the caverns lie empty once again.
(Photo: courtesy of Tony Pearce)

Cambrian Quarry, Gwernymynydd, 1978

In the hillside behind the Rainbow Inn lies a silica mine worked during the 1940s and 50s. Part of the mine was later used for disposing of poor quality carbon black dust by the Ellesmere Port company Cabot Carbon. Several companies later tried, without success, to retrieve the carbon black by using vacuum pipes only to discover, the hard way, why Cabot put it there.

The mine was a small series of chambers with supporting pillars, but several have now collapsed. Mined stone was conveyed to surface via a tunnel with its entrance beside the main Mold road. Several chambers are floored with loose carbon dust up to a foot deep. Even the most gentle of footsteps create great black clouds which rise in slow motion, coating every pore of the skin and requiring several soapy baths to remove.

In recent years some surface quarrying has been carried out on a small scale.

Lloyd`s Spar Mine, Hendre, 1982

This mine overlooks the Mold-Denbigh road, lying close to the Royal Oak at Hendre. It comprised about a mile of roomy passages and chambers descending to a depth of about 60 metres. It worked a 6 metre wide vein of spar or calcite. The vein runs south from Hendre and has been worked at three points along its length before eventually terminating in the River Alyn Valley, close to Pantymwyn at the popularly known Devil`s Gorge.   >>>>>
(Photo: courtesy of Martin Lloyd)

Lloyd`s Spar Mine, Hendre

Mining began at this site in the 1930s, the spar mined being used for pebble-dash. The photo shows the width of the vein containing the spar. The view looks down onto the lowest level in the mine.

The venture finally closed in 1984 when cheap imports of the material from Greece and Spain made mining uneconomical. When the pumps were eventually turned off, the lower section of the mine quickly flooded.

(Photo: courtesy of Martin Lloyd)

Limestone Mine at Hendre

Known by miners as "The Quarry"

During the 1940s, 50s and 60s, the lead company Halkyn District United Mines at Hendre diversified by mining high quality limestone at the request of the Ministry of Agriculture. The stone was initially used as an ingredient in fertiliser, but most of the output in later years went to Pilkingtons' of St Helens for glass making. The stone was mined from a depth of 120 metres below the hamlet of Hendre and raised to surface at the nearby Olwyn Goch Shaft. Halkyn Mines also mined smaller quantities of limestone from a depth of nearly 250 metres near Pen-y-Bryn Shaft on Halkyn Mountain.

Limestone was extracted at the rate of 70,000 to 80,000 tonnes a year and consequently created some impressive workings. If placed end to end, the chambers and passages would total over two miles in length. The ventilation of such large chambers created some problems and blasting was normally done at the end of each shift to allow fumes to disperse. For the same reason battery locos were used in this area whereas diesel locos were used in the main tunnel. The picture above shows the chamber numbered "3/2 West" on old plans.

2. SLATE MINES

The slate mines of Clwyd lie chiefly in the Corwen, Llangollen and Chirk areas, the largest being those known as Penarth, Moel Fferna and Cambrian Quarries. The size of their waste tips gives some idea of the underground extent of the workings although only one tenth of the mined material ended up as finished product.

The material was first worked in Wales at least since the time of the Romans, but this is thought to have been on a very limited scale. More recently the arrival of the railways coincided with an increasing demand for roofing slates, particularly in the domestic market of the growing industrial towns of the North. Production reached its height in the 1890s. Most local slate mines began life as quarries. They later developed into underground enterprises as the dipping slate beds were followed deeper into the often remote hillsides.

Although some quarries produced slate of inferior quality, no roofing material has been found to match top grade slate. It is both waterproof and extremely durable. However, short-termism demands cheaper alternatives. As a result, Clwyd's last slate mine was wound up in 1960.

Penarth Quarry, near Corwen
Main haulage incline to surface

Also known as Corwen Slate Mine, it lies on the slopes of the Berwyn Hills, its tips clearly visible from the A5 on the hillside a mile or two south-east of Corwen. Slate was conveyed by steeply inclined tramway, down to the main line railway in the valley below. The underground workings are fairly extensive and were developed on three different levels, slate being raised to surface up railed inclines as shown above. The most productive years of Penarth spanned from 1870 until its closure in 1932.

Moel Ferna Mine, Glyndyfrdwy
Marshalling Yard, Floor 5

Similar in character to Penarth and exploiting the same beds of slate, Moel Ferna also lies on the slopes of the Berwyns but a little closer to Llangollen. A long rough track leads up the hill to the site but this has weathered into a footpath since the mine closed. The derelict mine buildings and view over the Dee Valley far below combine to create an almost mystical atmosphere. It is easy to imagine the ghosts of the old miners toiling away as they would in days gone by. The marshalling yard above once housed extensive sidings for the narrow gauge wagons. Although the floor appears solid, the right-hand side is in fact supported on steelwork which forms part of the roof of a large lower chamber.   >>>>>
(Photo: Jon Knowles)

Moel Ferna Mine
Chain Suspension Bridge on level 4

Work began at Moel Ferna in the 1860s and it was the last of the working Clwyd slate mines, eventually closing in 1960. The extensive workings are almost entirely below ground. Loaded wagons reached the main line railway in the valley below by means of a long narrow-gauge incline. They were simply powered by gravity, being controlled by a riding brakesman, presumably with nerves of steel.

The suspension bridge above was constructed over a 20 metre drop to provide direct access from the main level to surface. >>>>>

Moel Ferna Mine

Entrances are frequently the most unstable sections of a mine. In the instance above our party of explorers had walked up the hillside to the only other entrance. Here we abseiled down an 18 metre shaft pulling the rope down after us expecting to be able to walk out of the main adit below. Unfortunately the passage had collapsed and the only negotiable way out was completely blocked. We should have checked this entrance was clear beforehand! Luckily within an hour or two of taking this photograph, a crawl had been excavated through the collapse and the party made it to daylight.

3.   COLLIERIES

The Industrial Revolution, it is said, could not have occurred, as it did, without Britain's enormous reserves of coal. These allowed our country to lead the world with the technologies of the time, up until the start of the twentieth century. The history of Clwyd coal mining goes back more than 600 years to when shallow seams were exploited close to the shores of the Dee Estuary. In more recent times, dozens of collieries once dotted the lowland landscapes of the Mostyn, Bagillt, Mold, Llay, Gresford and Ruabon areas. A Royal Commission in 1905 estimated the coal reserves of Denbighshire alone to amount to almost 100,000,000 tons. The same county in 1914 employed over 12,000 coal miners.

The story of coal mining may be one of success and riches, but this was only achieved at the expense of the miner who was frequently treated with appalling disregard by mine-owners. The history of mining tells of countless disputes, strikes and riots merely in hope of fair treatment and improved working conditions. The second half of the twentieth century marked the decline and eventual closure of the industry due to industrial change, foreign competition and political will.

Vron Colliery near Wrexham

This photo, taken around 1900, is typical of the many small local collieries of the time.

Vron Colliery began life in 1806 overlooking the village of Tan-y-Fron. It was owned in 1850 by a Mr. Low of Wrexham, who became well known as one vof the promoters of the original Channel Tunnel Scheme for which offices were opened in Wrexham! Little did they know that it would be a further 140 years before their plan was to be completed. The mine employed 330 men in 1914 but finally closed during the depression of 1930.

(From an old postcard)

The Gresford Colliery Disaster

Gresford was a comparatively recent colliery on the outskirts of Wrexham which was first begun in 1907. It was worked via the Dennis Shaft and the Martin Shaft, both over 700 metres deep. In the early 1930s it employed around 2,200 men. But at 2 o`clock on the morning of 22nd September 1934 one of Britain's worst colliery disasters occurred.

An explosion in the Dennis section of the mine was followed by an extensive fire in the main intake airway. A total of 262 miners and 3 rescuers lost their lives. Only a handful escaped. The fire was fought continuously until the evening of the following day by which time it was certain that all must be dead. A unanimous decision of mine owners, workmen and H.M.Inspectors then resolved to seal off the mine at the shaft tops.

Further explosions followed, one of which destroyed one of the shaft cappings and killed a nearby worker, thus making a total of 266 fatalities. Only 11 bodies were recovered. The photo shows the only surface relic left standing in 1978. Sadly even this is now gone. >>>>>

Source: Report by Parry Davies, Captain of the rescue team. His report forms part of the Gresford Colliery Disaster Relief Fund manuscripts at Flintshire Record Office (Ref: D/GF).

Gresford Colliery

A Court of Inquiry published its report in 1937. Their findings disclosed the fact that the Coal Mines Regulation Act of 1908 had largely been ignored by workmen, shot-firers, deputies and management alike. Men had been asked to work beyond the legal maximum shift hours and more crucially, standard practices regarding ventilation had not been carried out. As a result of the report, legal proceedings were taken out that year against owners, management and staff of the colliery. 43 charges were laid. Fines in respect of only 8 were imposed totalling £140 with £350 costs. All remaining charges were dismissed or withdrawn.

Following much repair work in the adjoining part of the mine, the colliery re-opened in January 1936, and by 1939 was employing 2000 men and back in full production. The photo above is thought to show a section of the re-opened part of the mine some years later.

Point of Ayr Colliery

Point of Ayr was the last to close of the many North Wales collieries. It began operations under this name back in 1887. Three shafts gave access to the seams, the deepest being 336 metres. The most recent workings extended northeast under the sea for two miles. At one time up to 60 ponies were stabled below ground for haulage.

Coal mines generally suffer from instability problems due to the nature of the seams and this photo shows what can happen when the surrounding strata decide to make a move. Note that some allowance has been made for this movement, as the vertical girders are connected to the roof girders by means of hinges and not fixed bolts. >>>>>

(Photo: RJB Mining)

22

Point of Ayr

The mine was known as a "gassy" mine, with methane being normally extracted at a rate of up to 500 litres a second. The mine had its own independent electricity generating plant comprising five large English Electric generators designed to run on diesel or methane from the mine. Each could provide up to 700 kilowatts. After 1968, electricity was purchased from the National Grid, the requirement prior to closure being 3700 kW.

This photo shows the difficulties involved when mining through bad ground. Rock bolting proved inadequate and the more traditional hydraulic jacks have been installed. Note how the forest of equipment and hydraulic pipes makes the route almost impassable. >>>>>

Source: NCB information leaflet

(Photo: RJB Mining)

23

Point of Ayr

Point of Ayr did much of the pioneering work on the rock bolting technique of roof support. Instead of the standard form of hydraulic supports, long rods would be anchored deep into the surrounding rock. The main advantages were those of increased working space and economy. Rock bolting was highly successful and led to a period of record production.

This cutting machine demonstrates the advantage of an increased working space. Consider that this huge vehicle was assembled entirely underground in "kit" form and that all parts had to be lowered laboriously down the shaft in the small cages.

Sadly, after a life of over 100 years, the mine finally closed in August 1996. Salvage work was carried out for a further 18 months then the shafts were sealed and the pumps switched off. The last remaining headgear was blasted down in July 1997.

Farewell to the last mine of any kind to work in Clwyd.

(Photo: courtesy of Martin Pitt, photographer)

4.   LEAD MINES

Lead mining has had a dramatic effect upon the social and economic structure of the area. From the year 1700 to 1870 it provided the main form of employment. Only the lead mining areas of Yorkshire and Derbyshire exceeded Clwyd in productivity. The limestone area between Prestatyn in the north and Llangollen in the south is criss-crossed with veins of lead. Many of these showed at the surface where the ore could be seen as gashes in cliff faces. These are the veins which were worked first by the Romans, if not earlier, and were consequently fairly shallow affairs.

As ore was removed and the workings became deeper, so flooding became a problem; one that dogged the industry for most of its history. This was a very wet mining area and many schemes were introduced to keep the working face free from water. In early days "rag and chain" pumps were used which simply raised water by dragging rags up through a wooden tube, but this method cannot have been too effective. In the early 1700s, mines at Loggerheads, near Mold, had numerous wind pumps in operation, which presumably limited production to blowy periods. A more successful method was the construction of drainage adits or tunnels cut into a hillside to intersect a mine at its lowest point, which allowed water to drain off naturally. But it wasn't long before the mines had been worked below these adits. Salvation, at least for a while, came in the form of what eventually developed into the Cornish Pumping Engine. These huge stationary steam beam engines housed in great stone engine houses, raised heavy timber rods up and down deep shafts to power the pumps below. By 1870 the area had hundreds of these machines in operation, many wetter mines employing several. Eventually, the high cost of keeping water from the mines combined with the influx of cheap imported ore led to the industry's demise.

One or two mines managed to keep going. The most notable of these being Halkyn District United Mines. During the 1930s this company made profits at a time of great depression when all other mines were closing. This was only possible due to a deep drainage adit, the Milwr Tunnel, which was driven from the Dee Estuary at Bagillt and was first begun in 1897. By 1930 the tunnel face had reached an area beneath Halkyn Mountain and as a result provided drainage for all the veins of the area down to sea-level. Many mining companies had previously amalgamated to finance the enormous costs of driving the tunnel, which eventually terminated near Loggerheads, 10 miles from the entrance at Bagillt. This approach ensured good profits from lead for the company until almost 1960.

Local caving clubs and mine enthusiasts have worked hard in the last 30 years to preserve many of the areas underground workings. Little remains of the industry on the surface, except a handful of stone engine houses and a few rare relics. Perhaps the best known legacy is the landscape. Thousands of old shaft craters remain, particularly in the areas of Minera and Halkyn and some shafts are still open. Even these landscape features are threatened by the many reclamation schemes already started or planned for the near future. Only when the entire area has been bulldozed and seeded may authorities begin to realise what they have destroyed. A glimmer of hope lies in the fact that, in the last few years, professional archaeologists are beginning to treat such remains with the importance they deserve while a number of studies have been carried out to monitor what remains.

The Hush Vein at Eisteddfod near Minera

This 1991 aerial photograph shows the extent to which a vein can be exploited at the surface. Hundreds of shaft and pit type excavations can be seen along the line of the vein which runs from the top right down towards the bottom left of the picture. The village of Gwynfryn can just be seen at the top left-hand side with Minera quarry at the top right.

This vein may have been worked by the Romans 2000 years ago but much of the ancient evidence is likely to have been obliterated by the generations of miners who have followed in their footsteps.

Some survey work has been carried out over the last few years by the Clwyd-Powys Archaeological Trust in this area. Although their report is not freely available to the public it identifies the mining area as being unique in Wales and worthy of preservation.

(Crown copyright: RCAHMW)

Shaft Sealing, Halkyn Mountain, 1978

Although the majority of lead mine shafts in the area may have collapsed or been filled long ago, there remained hundreds that were still open and possibly in a dangerous condition. Since 1978 there have been a number of schemes which attempted to tackle this problem. The quickest (and cheapest) method shown above, involved placing a prefabricated steel cage over the open shaft, then cementing stones over the cage. The main drawback, however, was that this method could only offer a temporary solution. Most of these old shafts had internal dry stone walling which was often built upon a timber collar at a depth of say 10 or 15 metres. Eventually the collar will rot, the walling could collapse and a crater or an open hole would once again appear. This also explains why so many "new" holes continue to appear throughout the area.

The most successful, but more costly, method involved excavating the shaft down to solid rock. A steel plate could then be laid on the rock and thick cement poured on top. This method was used successfully on hundreds of shafts in the early 1980s.

The Dig

The modern mining enthusiast is required to possess many skills, especially when digging out a blocked or collapsed shaft in the hope of entering extensive "new" workings. General engineering, joinery and metalworking knowledge is combined with specialist skills such as narrow gauge railway construction and a thorough knowledge of obscure reference books such as 'Shaft Sinking Through Running Sand'.

Normally old records and plans are scrutinised to assess the potential of a site but in the case opposite, in woods at Aberduna Farm near Maeshafn, no records could be found. Despite this, a dig was begun where it appeared that an old shaft had collapsed and was filled to the surface. It was also thought that the only drainage adit for this mine ran directly beneath, just 12 metres down. Large quantities of timber and materials were carried to the site, a hand winch built over the spot, a 12 inch gauge railtrack and wagon were constructed to carry the spoil away then digging, or shaft sinking, commenced. Despite the extensive work involved, no workings were found at this particular site and the dig was abandoned. From the initial stages of the project it was affectionately known amongst cavers as 'The Great No-hoper'.

The Descent

This shows a once common method of entering old lead mines involving cavers' 'electron' ladders and a lifeline rope. This shaft at Eryrys, known as Mary Anne Shaft on Bog Mine, was 190 metres deep before it was capped in the 1980s. Cavers have explored passages at depths of up to 100 metres here, but below this level the workings are now flooded. Most cavers limit the depth climbed on ladder to about 100 metres due to the exertion involved.

Today, most deep descents are tackled using Single Rope Techniques which involve abseiling to descend and mechanical jamming devices to ascend. This method can be faster and less exhausting if done correctly, but without the safety measure of a separate lifeline, dependence upon equipment is total.

Westminster Mine, Eryrys

When explorers have managed to get underground, further work is frequently required. Here, in this 1820s passage, a collapse from above blocked the passage completely with mud and boulders. Initially digging was not possible as there was no space to put the excavated material nearby. A light-gauge railway was therefore constructed to tram the waste to where it could be tipped down a 65 metre shaft into a sump. Material for the dig had to be carried into the mine via a flat-out crawl and a flooded passage. The tubing along the passage floor is the syphon pipe which drained off this water before the team could work at the dig.

Belgrave Mine near Llanferres

Many local caving and mining enthusiasts offer to become a part of the long-established North Wales Cave Rescue Organisation. This group of volunteers ensure that in the very rare case of an accident, their rescuers are usually their friends. Here the NWCRO are about to haul a stretcher-case up a small internal shaft deep in the mine.

Consider that one rope is required to haul the stretcher, a second as a stretcher safety line, a caving ladder is also required for the man who must accompany the stretcher on its ascent and he must be life-lined by a third rope. Consequently a common problem at rescues is that space is not available for the many team members required to do the hauling. Observing the ensuing difficulties acts as a good deterrent to team members thinking of being rescued in the future!

North Hendre Mine

This is an example of what the old miners were looking for. In the roof of this passage is a narrow vein of lead ore which, in this case, was too meagre and therefore uneconomical to extract. Typical lead veins could vary from a few centimetres to a metre or more in width.

Most of the ore found in this mine was not found in a vein of this kind, but in what were known as "flats". Here the ore was found in large lumps in clay-filled almost horizontal passages. A number of rich local mines exploited similar such flats. Amongst these were Rhosesmor, East-Halkyn, Fron Fownog near Cadole, and Pant-y-Gof Mine at Halkyn.   >>>>>

(Photo: Graham Woolley)

North Hendre Mine

An old compressed-air powered drum winch dated from about 1880.

This mine was severely hampered by flooding. Although powerful water pumps were operated, the mine was forced to close on numerous occasions. This winch was used to raise heavy pumps from the deepest part of the mine, up an inclined passage, whenever the water level rose. The winch was originally mounted on timbers a metre or two above the floor, but now lies where it fell, due to the effects of dry rot.

Ponies were used for haulage in one area of the mine and were stabled underground. This was unusual for local lead mines. The stabling room which is shown on old plans still exists below ground but, despite several attempts, cavers have not yet managed to get through the collapsed passage which leads to this area.

(Photo: Graham Woolley)

The Holywell Boat Level

This was an important early drainage adit begun in 1774 from a point close to the well at Holywell. By 1879 it was nearly a mile long and ran almost parallel to the old A55 road in the direction of Lloc. It was important because it drained a number of different veins intersected along its length, including Brammock's, Partridge, the Pant-y-Nef and the eastern end of the Old Holway Vein. An unusual feature of this adit was that at one time it conveyed ore to the surface on floating barges which were propelled by a man lying on his back upon the cargo and "walking" along the roof.
(Photo: Chris Williams)

The Park Day Level, Minera

The Minera Lead Mines were much troubled by large quantities of water which entered from natural cave systems nearby.   The Park Day Level was one of several adits driven into the same mine. It was begun around 1766 but has been repaired and extended many times. This nicely brick-lined section is not far from the portal and still has the narrow gauge rails laid along the floor. At times of heavy rain, enormous quantities of water from Minera Mountain surge through this passage making all access impossible.   >>>>>

The Park Day Level

Much of this adit runs through good solid rock and is self-supporting. Only where the roof has been unstable has the tunnel been reinforced with brick lining. About a mile up the tunnel a large collapse had blocked the way for modern explorers. Undaunted, a long-term dig was begun which involved bringing heavy pre-cast concrete supports from a quarter of a mile down the tunnel up to the working face, where they were erected to allow digging to take place safely. The photo above shows the dig just at the time when the break-through was made. However, as so often occurs, a much larger collapse was found some distance beyond this point and another dig was abandoned. >>>>>

The Park Day Level

To carry out the work of excavating through such a collapse it was necessary to re-construct the original narrow gauge railway, which at this end of the tunnel had been dismantled. Sleepers, rail and rolling stock were manufactured then installed to provide almost a quarter of a mile of working tramway. This was needed to enable the heavy lintels to be transported to the face and to carry waste from the dig back to the nearest part of the passage with enough room for dumping. The joy of their labours can be seen upon the faces of the resting crew.

The Halkyn Tunnel

This is Clwyd`s second longest lead mines drainage adit and was started in 1818. It runs for 5 miles from a point a mile or so west of Flint, nearly to Pant-y-Mwyn west of Mold, but since the closure of the mines it has collapsed at a number of points. This tunnel was a great success in draining many mines along its route, most of which had previously been abandoned due to flooding. The tunnel passed directly beneath the secret government site at Rhydymwyn and was linked to the surface by shafts which lay within its perimeter fence. There was no direct connection between the secret government chambers built into the hillside and the mines beneath.
(Photo: Jerry Dobby/Mike Gannon)

The Halkyn Tunnel

More recent explorations deep into Halkyn Mountain have revealed a labyrinth of old workings dating back 150 years or more. Many artifacts remain which add not only to cavers' understanding of mining technology but also to the atmosphere of the now silent passages.

These two pictures show differing aspects of the Halkyn Tunnel where it passes through unstable ground. Stabilising work was carried out in the 1950s to safeguard the water supply which flowed from the entrance near Flint. In the lower picture, the supports made from cast-iron pipe and rail track are original. They were put in place where this branch of the tunnel passes beneath the present day Tiger Tim factory at Rhosesmor. To reach this area involves a five mile return trip through old workings.

Beneath Halkyn Mountain

Part of modern day exploration often involves climbing in old workings to reach `new` passages above. In this example, explorers used battery-powered drills and rock bolts to scale a vertical height of 60 metres to reach a major passage indicated on old mine plans. Unfortunately the passage was not found at the expected position on the first attempt: it took three attempts at drilling routes of over 60 metres before the 'black hole' was eventually found and entered. The picture was taken looking directly down the open stope from the 'new' passage and shows one of the first of the recent explorers as he abseils down.

Halkyn Mines Relics

Generally, when veins are worked out, machinery is removed for use elsewhere. However, a surprising number of artifacts still remain scattered throughout the workings of Halkyn Mines.

The pump (upper photo) was found in Rhosesmor Mine at the bottom of Batter's Shaft and was thought to have been used to pump to the surface where water for processing was scarce. There are several other larger pumps in these workings.

The Drill Carriage (lower photo) was found in a high level passage of Lode 621. It was designed to be transported through the mine by rail on its own wheels. After removal of the wheels it could then be braced between floor and roof where a drilling machine would have been fixed to the arm ready for drilling.

Although this is a heavy machine, another has recently been found in higher workings which is considerably heavier. Both date from around 1900 -1910.

The Milwr Tunnel

Clwyd's longest and most impressive drainage adit was begun in 1897 from sea-level at Bagillt. It is now 10 miles long and ends at Cadole, near Loggerheads. It drains over 50 veins and creates a labyrinth of interconnected passages totalling over 60 miles in length. The successful drainage of so many veins allowed profits to be made at a time when most other lead mines had closed. During the 1930s, up to 650 men were employed by the mine; European and World tunneling records were being broken. Note the flood levels indicated by staining on the passage wall. A metre deep trench beneath the floor timbers carries the water out into the Dee Estuary. >>>>>
(Photo: Bob Roberts)

The Milwr Tunnel - Rhosesmor Branch

Almost mid-way along the 10 mile Milwr Tunnel, a branch passage was driven east to drain the mines of the Rhosesmor area. This tunnel in 1931 broke into a large natural cavern in Powell's Lode.

This recent photograph shows a 'man-rider' used to convey the workforce to the working area at change of shift. Many other items of rolling stock remain in the workings today. Amongst them are two diesel locos, three battery locos, three man-riders and a large assortment of mine wagons.

(Photo: Nick Catford)

The Milwr Tunnel

All good things it seems, come to an end and lead mining from the Milwr Tunnel was scaled down radically after the 1960s. One of the last lodes to be worked for lead was Lode 524, previously known as the Pant-y-Buarth Vein. The photo shows some of the small workforce of 10 men working on this lode in 1978. Not long after this, they stopped mining lead ore completely and the men were kept busy with shaft capping work and tunnel maintenance until final closure in 1987. >>>>>
(Photo: Chris Williams)

The Milwr Tunnel Portal

Although all lead mining has now ended, the tunnel continues to disgorge large volumes of water, normally around 1.2 Cubic metres per second (23 million gallons per day) which rises to 1.9 cubic metres per second (36 million gallons per day) in wet weather. For many years Halkyn District United Mines, who owned the tunnel, were partly owned by the textile firm Courtaulds who used this abundant and cheap water for their processing. Although Courtaulds closed a few years ago the water is still piped to new industries at Flint.

Engine Houses

Many impressive stone-built engine houses once dotted the mining areas of Clwyd. They housed large steam "Cornish" pumping engines which operated huge cast-iron beams which lifted moved heavy wooden pump rods up and down the adjacent shafts. This reciprocating movement was sufficient to power large underground pumps and keep the work-place free of water. Some wet mines had several of these engines operating simultaneously, resulting in raising perhaps 750 litres (166 gallons) per second. To give an indication of the size of these Cornish engines, the diameter of their single cylinders could be as much as 2.5 metres. Today only a handful of these buildings remain; all the Cornish engines themselves having been removed for scrap long ago. The most complete buildings are those of Clive Shaft at Dyserth, Pennant Mine at Rhuallt, the Engine Shaft at Hendre Mine, Brymbo Colliery, Nant Engine Shaft near Eryrys and City Shaft at Minera.

Industrial archaeologists are currently considering the fate of one or two of these. The engine house at Pennant Mine is currently undergoing a restoration programme and City Shaft engine house has been significantly restored and its location made into a mining heritage site. The photo opposite shows the reconstruction work in progress around 1994.

(Photo: Selwyn Edwards)

Minera Mines

Streams can be found in many local mines, particularly in wet weather. Here a stream cascades down a passage which passes directly beneath the surface river of Afon Sychnant. Flooding is often considered by the public to be a primary risk to the modern caver, although in Clwyd there are only a few sites which suffer from flash flooding. Most wet sites have a tendency to fill up slowly in wet weather and do not normally threaten the unwary, but they might!   >>>>>
(Photo: Selwyn Edwards)

Minera Mines

At one time there were many different lead mines at Minera, working several different veins. The most extensive complex lay south-east of the large, now disused, limestone quarry near the hamlet of Gwynfryn.

Due to constant flooding problems a number of companies eventually amalgamated to form the Minera Mining Company which enabled deep drainage tunnels to be financed. In later years Minera Mines became a major producer of zinc ore. The disused workings that remain are a three dimensional labyrinth which extends for miles.

At several points, shafts connect with the surface and provide routes for natural ventilation. Opposite, icicles have formed deep underground due to the combination of bitter cold on the surface and strong ventilation.

(Photo: Selwyn Edwards)

48

5.   BONE CAVES

Long before pot-holers were invented, caves were examined, mainly in the 1800s by archaeologists both amateur and professional. They sought evidence of ancient mammals and early man. It was a boom time for anyone with a trowel, a sieve and the inclination.

Many of Clwyd's caves were completely blocked with clays, forced into them by receding glaciers. Archaeologists dug at such sites removing, in some cases, thousands of tonnes of infill. Today's professional archaeologists rely heavily upon technology, funding and not least the work of amateurs who are frequently responsible for identifying the sites in the first place but rarely get mentioned in dispatches. From the work of such people, we now know that Clwyd Man freely roamed the area as long as 230,000 years ago. We also have ample evidence from many Clwyd caves of the existence of wolf, wild boar, hyaena, lion, bear, rhinoceros, hippopotamus, elephant and mammoth.

Despite past activity, the future for cave archaeology in Clwyd is bright and there is much more to learn from the remaining undisturbed deposits. Most known bone caves have only been partly excavated and some are untouched. There is little doubt that an even greater number remain undiscovered for the archaeologists of the future.

Entrance to Ffynnon Beuno Cave, Tremeirchion

The picture above shows one of a small cluster of bone caves first excavated in the 1880s by Mr Luxmore and Mr Hicks. Amongst the bones they found were those of wolf, wild boar, cave bear, cave lion, straight-tusked elephant and woolly mammoth. Also found were artifacts indicating human occupation over 3000 years ago. There are about fifty known archaeological caves in Clwyd and 'new' ones are still occasionally being discovered.

A glacially sealed un-excavated cave near Denbigh

This shows a likely archaeological cave prior to any excavation work taking place. In this case, the original entrance measures 5 metres by 3 metres. Movement of passing glaciers causes such caves to become entirely sealed with clay and materials forced in from the entrance. Mixed with the clay of this cave are large lumps of disturbed stalagmite which must once have adorned the floor of an impressive cave passage. The author excavated a small trial trench in front of the entrance in the 1970s in an attempt to establish the depth of the cave floor. This site requires a long-term, large-scale, professional excavation to yield its secrets.

Pont Newydd Cave, Cefn, St.Asaph

Of all the archaeological caves in Clwyd, Pont Newydd Cave contains the oldest known human remains.

It was originally excavated by Professor William Boyd-Dawkins, author of "Cave Hunting", in 1874. Although Boyd-Dawkins paid labourers by the ton excavated, he still managed to find the only evidence, at that time, of Palaeolithic man in North Wales. A major dig from 1978 by the National Museum of Wales confirmed human remains as being 230,000 years old, one of only two such sites in Britain. Remains of an adult and two children were found. As a bonus the Boyd-Dawkins waste tips were re-examined and found to contain various items of interest including many stone hand axes.

The photo shows archaeologists in action, if that's not a contradiction in terms, during the 1978 excavations.

(Photo: courtesy of the National Museum of Wales)

6.   SPORTING CAVES

Caving in Britain began to attract attention around the beginning of the 20th century, when people started descending some of the deep 'pots' of the Yorkshire Moors and Derbyshire Dales. North Wales was only regarded as an area of archaeological importance, the longest known cave being 150 metres, and most of that had been excavated at the end of the 19th century. It was not until the 1950s that the area began to receive a more determined examination, from those with a belief that large caves were waiting to be discovered. Since that time cavers have doggedly dug, crawled, squeezed and swum into hundreds of "new" caves, most of which had never before been seen by man. Most of these discoveries tend to be of very modest proportions, but once in a while a major cave is found. It may be half a mile in length or as long as three miles, as in the case of Ogof Pool Parc at Minera in 1986.

The modern caver is an eternal optimist. He spends most of his time and effort, often fruitlessly, digging holes in the ground, 'knowing' that one of them, one day, will break into 'caverns measureless to man'. Caving today remains one of the few activities which offers the ordinary man or woman a chance to be a true pioneer and to tread where no person has trod before. It all lies on the doorstep, just under your feet.

Opposite, an image of an early caver
taken from an old postcard.

Photo

W. *Burrows*

FIG. 29.   CAVE EXPLORER, WITH GAS LAMP

A promising site on Minera Mountain

One method of finding a new cave: first find a stream flowing over limestone which disappears in a blind valley, as above.

Next, dig down through boulders and mud. Finally, continue digging for as long as it takes!

Some caves require very little work to reveal their secrets, but normally discoveries only occur after long-term projects involving hundreds of man-hours. The stream above disappears underground amongst boulders and is typical of the sites sought by cavers to begin a new dig. The sinking water is now known to enter the three mile long cave of Ogof Pool Parc.

Ogof Noeth, near World's End

Ogof Noeth was discovered in 1984. A few boulders were pulled from a hole on the moors, then hammering removed some awkward corners to allow human access for the first time. Ogof Noeth translates as Naked Cave, as it was necessary to strip off to squeeze through the tight entrance. A cave 150 metres long lies beyond the entrance, but the entire route is a flat-out crawl. Further work by thin cavers is likely to extend the length of this cave considerably.

Gas Pot, Minera Mountain

Many cave digs are abandoned before any discoveries can be made, often due to limited potential or lack of will. Others like Gas Pot are continued until they become substantial engineering projects. This was begun at a point where surface flood waters sink into fissures in the ground. Excavated from the surface, it's current depth is almost 40 metres thus making it one of Britains deepest excavated cave digs. Over 3000 man-hours have been spent here, involving several tons of timber and scaffolding. Digging continues sporadically but optimism is beginning to wane.

(Right photo: Graham Woolley)

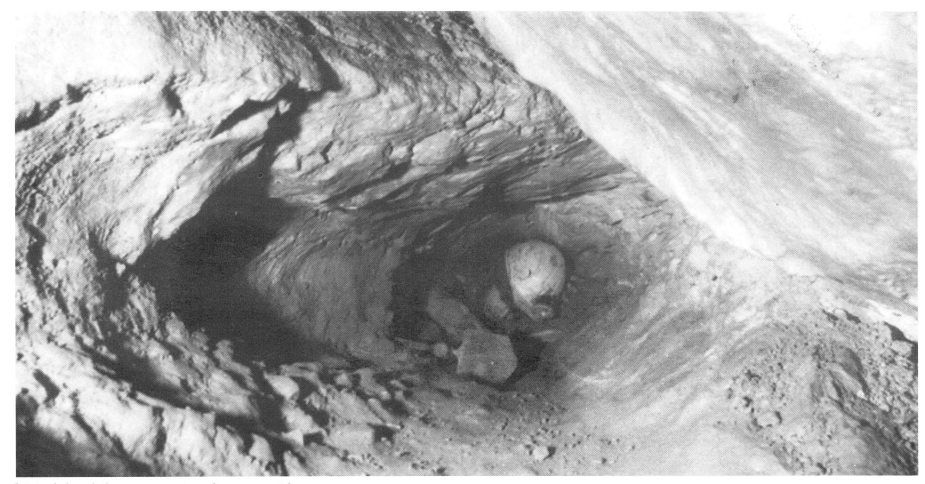

Ogof Nadolig (Christmas Cave), near Cilcain
"The Blasted Crawl"

A more familiar method of locating new cave passages might be that of negotiating a squeeze. Many discoveries have been the result of pushing through tight passages, but in this case the squeeze was created by two days work with a Kango drill. By using a generator on the surface and laying cables through the cave it was possible to drill shot holes and blast, to enlarge a rabbit-sized hole through which air was blowing. A short but interesting section of cave was found beyond.

Ogof Llyn Du, Minera

Water can be an obstacle to finding or extending caves. This passage leads to a deep sump from which only cave divers can explore. Despite very poor visibility, a series of dives has proved that the passage descends vertically below the surface for 25 metres then eventually surfaces after a length of 200 metres in a new cave of over half a mile in length. »»»»

Ogof Llyn Du

The exploration of caves particularly in North Wales, can be a messy business. There are many sites where the only way forward means wallowing in passages deep in liquid mud. This grubby-looking group typically fits the public perception of the modern caver. The wetsuits may provide warmth but they fail to prevent mud from penetrating where it should not! The photo was taken just after the cave's discovery in 1979.

Ogof Cefn-y-Gist, near World's End
Calcite Formations

Formations such as stalactites and stalagmites are not over-common in Clwyd's caves. They seem to be most abundant in the caves of the Minera area. Those shown above were found when the caver in the photo discovered a new passage by crawling under boulders in the floor. Although the length of this cave is only about 200 metres to the collapse at its end, dye put into the stream which flows through this cave has shown the water to re-emerge over 2.5 miles away. A large system waits to be discovered......

Ogof Dydd Byraf, Minera

This was the first major cave to be found in North Wales. Discovered close to a limestone quarry in 1964, it became the subject of a Public Inquiry when it was thought it might be destroyed. The total length of the cave is only half a mile, but it contains a fascinating variety of formations. The cave consists of a maze of passages, some 10 metres high, on three different levels and a large, now dry, river passage. >>>>>
(Photo: Bob Roberts)

Ogof Dydd Byraf

In the light of more recent discoveries in the area, it is now known that this cave forms only part of a much larger system, there being four caves which have now been proved to be linked. The whole system has an explored length of over 4 miles.

The passage shown above originally carried the river which formed Ogof Dydd Byraf in pre-glacial times.

'Poachers' Cave' near Cilcain
Also known as Ogof Hen Ffynnhonau

The Alyn Gorge contains a small cluster of interesting caves, most of which have been found by digging since 1974. Poachers' Cave is about half a mile in length and follows the underground River Alyn for much of this distance. During the summer months, the whole surface river is lost down swallow holes in the river bed and then follows a subterranean course through such caves. The water eventually finds its way into deep lead mine workings which take the water out into the Dee Estuary at Bagillt.   >>>>>
(Photo: Selwyn Edwards)

'Poachers' Cave'

The cave is about half a mile in length. Although the first few hundred metres involve crawling in a wide, mud floored passage, it then opens out at the junction with the main river passage. From here the route is mainly walking along an active stream bed, a rare treat in underground Clwyd.
Although the cave was discovered in the late 70s, flooding in recent years flushed away the mud blocking some of the lower passages and revealed new extensions. Although cavers have spent some time digging in this area, these extensions have not led to any major discoveries.
(Photo: Chris Williams)

Ogof Hesp Alyn, near Cilcain

This is the largest of the Alyn Gorge caves. One and a half miles have been explored since its discovery in 1974. It was discovered almost by chance, by cavers walking along the dry bed of the River Alyn on a warm summer's day. One of the group noticed vegetation moving at the river bank which, upon closer examination, was found to be due to a strong wind blowing up from a few boulders. This is always a promising indication of something interesting. Work began, boulders were hauled out, the dig grew deeper. At a depth of 9 metres, boulders in the floor gave way to reveal a passage of impressive dimensions. The digger at the bottom simply shouted up to the surface "I don't think we'll need the bucket any more".

Until mining lowered the water table in the 1920s, this cave was entirely flooded and its entrance was a spring. The cave has a vertical range of about 100 metres and is explored from the entrance downwards. Today, in times of severe flood, the cave will fill completely and again act as a spring. Not the place to be when it's too wet. The picture opposite shows a main passage in the cave where the route descends through large limestone boulders, some of which hang from the roof.   >>>>>

(Photo: Jerry Dobby)

Ogof Hesp Alyn

This cave was formed below the water table and the passages have been created chiefly by solution. Such passages are known as being 'phreatic' and frequently have a characteristically circular cross-section.

Opposite shows a phreatic passage where water flow direction can be ascertained from the shape of eroded eddy marks in the passage walls. An erosion-resistant thin calcite band can be seen running along the roof.

(Photo: Jerry Dobby)

Powell's Lode Cavern, Rhosesmor

An important group of Clwyd caves are those found within the lead mines. Numerous mining reports tell of the discovery of natural caverns, known to the local miners as 'Lochs' or 'Vughs'. Often these caverns seem to be isolated water-filled spaces formed by solution but, in the case of Powell's Lode Cavern at Rhosesmoor, the water flowing through it used to resurge at St Winefride`s Well at Holywell, five miles to the north, thus inferring a large unexplored cave system. Mining caused the well to dry up in 1917 and it is now supplied from a nearby mine`s drainage tunnel.by,

The photo opposite shows a small part of the chamber and lake formed at the intersection of two lead veins. The lake is known to be at least 60 metres in depth from which some 300 litres (66 gallons) per second overflow into the nearby Milwr Tunnel. The exact source of this water is unknown but much of it is likely to originate from the large catchment area of Halkyn Mountain.

Note the 'Tippler' beside the lake which emptied waste rock from mine wagons into the lake for many years without affecting water levels. >>>>>

(Photo: Nick Catford)

Powell's Lode Cavern

Here is another view of the cavern looking away from the lake. The rails in the distance enter a series of large natural caverns which extend horizontally for 300 metres before dipping below sea level. Although the route into these chambers is blocked, cavers have found an alternative route through old mine workings which by-pass the blockage. The pipes crossing in the foreground are simply to carry electricity cables clear of the wagons and rails. A maze of mine workings in this area extends upwards for over 125 metres to where a further large chamber named Arcadia, has recently been found.

The Underground Future

The majority of Clwyd's mines are likely to remain sealed, slowly deteriorating with the passage of time. The future lies chiefly in the hands of experienced amateur explorers who have already achieved much in terms of opening and preserving lead mines over the last 20 or 30 years, thus making them accessible to others. Professional archaeologists are now beginning to appreciate the secrets contained below ground from a mining history stretching back over 2000 years, but their interest seems likely to result in the exclusion, rather than the inclusion, of the public. Caves, on the other hand, will continue to be extended and new ones discovered by future generations of determined cavers. There are, for example, at least five cave systems known to exist in Clwyd which have not yet been entered by cavers, varying from half a mile and five miles in length. The problem lies in knowing exactly where, and for what distance, to dig. A cave guide book of 1967 listed 60 caves in Clwyd. The current total is around 250 and still rising...

Further Reading

(1980)   Metal Mines of North Wales   ISBN   1 872424 58 9
          by C.J.Williams (Revised edition 1997)

(1987)   Lead Mines of the Alyn Valley   ISBN   0 9512776 0 X
          by C.J.Williams

(1989)   Limestones & Caves of Wales   ISBN   0 521 32438 6
          edited by Trevor D. Ford (Pages 217 to 254)

(1991)   A Gazeteer of the Welsh Slate Industry   ISBN   0 86381 196 5
          by Alun John Richards

(1991)   Ice Age Hunters   ISBN   0 7200 0358X
          by S. Green & E. Walker (on the Bone Caves of
          Wales)

(1993)   The Milwr Tunnel: Bagillt to Loggerheads   ISBN   0 9522242 0 8
          by Cris Ebbs

(1995)   Minera: Lead Mines & Quarries   ISBN   0 952 55 29 0 6
          Edited by John Bennett

Index of sites illustrated

About the author

Cris Ebbs was born in Liverpool in 1947. Following a naval education at H.M.S. Conway officer training school, and a short time at sea with Manchester Liners, he has had a varied career which included 10 years in the jewellery trade, during which time he managed shops in Liverpool and St.Ives in Cornwall. For 20 years he has been a service engineer and now runs his own small business.

It was during his time in St.Ives that he was consumed by a passion for all things speleological. Since then he has been caving for 25 years throughout Britain, Ireland, France and Spain. Cris is a member of the Northern Mines Research Society, the Council for British Archaeology (Wales), the Welsh Mines Society and the Clwyd based Grosvenor Caving Club. In 1993 he published his first book "The Milwr Tunnel" describing the history of one of the country's longest lead mine tunnels.